MARRIAGE MAKEOVER

Your One Month Complete Guide
To A Brand New Home

SAM ORE

ALSO BY SAM ORE

PURPOSE REDEFINED:
LEVERAGING YOUR CORE INTELLIGENCE
FOR GLOBAL IMPACT

THIS GOSPEL REVOLUTION:
UNVEILING JESUS AND THE COMING GLORY

TOWARDS A PURPOSEFUL MARRIAGE:
PRACTICAL GUIDES FOR THE SINGLES

EMPOWERED

THE PARTY HAPPY GOD

COPYRIGHT

This publication may not be reproduced, stored in a retrieval system, or transmitted in whole or part, in any form or by any means, electronic, mechanical, photo copying, recording, or otherwise without print written permission of the publisher. All rights reserved solely by the author. The author guarantees all content are original and do not infringe upon the legal rights of any other person or work.

MARRIAGE MAKEOVER:
Your One Month Complete Guide
To A Brand New Home

Copyright © 2019

ISBN: 978-1-7327483-3-0

POWER COMMUNICATIONS
13011 Firestone Court
Silver Spring MD 20904

Dedication

This book is affectionately dedicated to my dear wife DEBBY ORE. My greatest achievement after coming back to the Trinitarian circle is my ability to convince you to marry me. Every day, I feel so privileged that you are my only wife and the only mother of our four Godly children. You are so sparklingly beautiful yet so humble in spirit. Your sacrifices in this marriage make me look like an expert on marriage and relationship.

When I brag on God's grace that you and I have never had a major dispute that we have not been able to resolve, it is because you prefer our peace to my militant disposition. But what you didn't know was that your willingness to take in all the combative tantrums because of my own insecurity will one day be used by God to teach me the way of grace. Now that I am having a better understanding of Christ and His finished work of grace, you have become the first recipient of my conversion. I love the way you graciously remind me in "cold sarcasms" when I occasionally display attitudes that are not Christ-like. "…I thought grace has also taken care of this…" to which I respond humorously "Sorry, I just relapsed into legalism."

I can truly say again and again that we are "stuck" in this covenant forever until we see Christ in glory. I love you so dearly. We give our heavenly Father all the praise.

Your hubby of 25 years and still counting,

Sam Ore

TABLE OF CONTENTS

Power Point 1:
Simplify The Vision For Your Marriage   14

Power Point 2:
Delete Traditions And Vain Philosophies   18

Power Point 3:
Grow In Your Love Walk   22

Power Point 4:
Choose Your Ministry/church Affiliation Wisely   26

Power Point 5:
Understanding Your Spouse's Dynamics   29

Power Point 6:
Pay Attention To Triangulation   34

Power Point 7:
Understanding Different Stages Of Marriage   38

Power Point 8:
Sacrificial Love: Husbands   44

Power Point 9:
Willing Submission: Wives   48

Power Point 10:
Say No To Comparison — 52

Power Point 11:
Marriage Physical Checkup — 56

Power Point 12:
Appreciate Your Spouse — 61

Power Point 13:
Understanding The Seasons Of Marriage — 64

Power Point 14:
Learn To Relax — 69

Power Point 15:
Understanding A Three-prong Communication — 73

Power Point 16:
Learning To Admire Your Spouse All Over Again — 77

Power Point 17:
Understanding True Forgiveness — 80

Power Point 18:
Be Intentional About Finacial Matters — 84

Power Point 19:
Learn To Speak Your Spouse's Language — 89

Power Point 20:
Develop Conflict Resolution Strategies — 93

Power Point 21:
Give No Place To Fear — 96

Power Point 22:
Learn To Give Up In Arguments — 100

Power Point 23:
Accept Who You Are In Christ   103

Power Point 24:
Maintain The Spirit Of Excellence   107

Power Point 25:
Maximize And Enjoy The Beauty Of Godly Sex   111

Power Point 26:
Appreciatig Your Extended Family   118

Power Point 27:
Understanding The Different Faces Of Your Spouse   121

Power Point 28:
Be Deliberate About Self-investment   125

Power Point 29:
Understanding The Stage Of Absorption   128

Power Point 30:
Go After Godly Mentors And Accountability Partners   132

Power Point 31:
Consider Intelligent Separation When Your Life Is
In Danger   139

Power Point 32:
Learn To Create Space For Your Spouse   139

Power Point 33:
Be Secured In God's Love   143

Power Point 34:
Be Alert In The Spirit   147

Introduction

A couple of months ago, I was having a conversation with a dear lady who told me "marriage is a scam." Noticing my surprise and agitation, she quickly added "…I am simply quoting a friend of mine who seems to have done everything to save her marriage without success." This simple, but rather harsh statement got me thinking. I started reflecting over hundreds of hours, if not thousands of hours, I have invested into counseling couples and singles alike from different cultures, backgrounds, and persuasions.

I have seen and heard different stories of woes, regrets, heartaches, broken hearts, and some that have led to the physical death of people in the relationship. But I have also seen happy, joyful couples thriving in their God-given purpose in life. The unfortunate thing though is that statistics are revealing that unless the tide is reversed, the marriage institution will suffer more tragic losses. The divorce rate is already at an all-time high. It is said that there is a divorce every 13 seconds in North America alone. Forty-nine percent of first marriage ends up in divorce. Second time marriage divorce rate is 62%, while third time marriage failure rate is 73%. This means that people keep making the same mistakes all over again. I am not a doom's day prophet or a Grim Reaper, but these are stats and facts conducted by psychologists and relationship experts (I reference them at the end of this book).

The average global divorce rate is arguably put at 50% by most studies. Although it varies from country to country depending on the cultures and the backgrounds of the couples involved. However, there is a surprising silver lining to these depressing statistics coming from the millennials. According to Bloomberg, "...Americans under the age of 45 have found a novel way to rebel against their elders. They are staying married." Divorce rates among them have declined by 18%. Some of the reasons associated with this trend are good education, focus and lessons from the older generation. Another reason that is attributed to this fact is that some of them are just simply co-habiting as married couples without any legal marriage documentations (you can't legally divorce someone if you were not married to the person in the first place).

There is another group within those who are still considered legally married. But the marriage is dead. They are the unhappy married couples. In other words, they are not happy and they feel trapped. Some of the reasons why they are still living together in "hell" revolve around fear of embarrassment should they divorce: It is humiliating to admit that they have failed. Some are still holding on because of the legal implications such as custody battle, child support, alimony, etc. Some other people, especially in Africa and the Middle East, hang in because of their children. Some unhappy couples just feel that they don't have a choice but to stay. Also, in certain cultures, it is seen as a terrible taboo to divorce. The social stigma on the couple and their families is almost like a curse. People will rather die in such marriages to save their families from shame.

Perhaps, the strongest reason why some people are still married is because of "eternal consequences of divorce." This is especially true of religious people brought up in environments with strict penal codes as a way of life. They believe that they will roast in hell forever if they ever divorce. The honest truth is that none of these reasons why people stay married is enough. All the reasons are still about emotional feelings, sentiments, and other people's opinions which are not inherently bad in themselves. But a closer look at each of them will truly reveal a faulty, egocentric mindset. At the end of the day, everything still comes back to the couple's fears and pride. Self-focus, self-obsession, is the number one reason if not the only main reason why many marriages fail.

This is why the main theme of this book is actually not about your spouse but about you and your personal relationship with Christ. When we focus on Christ and His finished work of grace and we allow the Holy Spirit to help us bear His fruit in us, guess what, our spouses will be the first to experience the beauty of God's grace at work in our lives. Just imagine for a few minutes, a man that is bearing the components of the fruit of the Spirit listed in Galatians 5:22 "...*But the fruit of the Spirit is love, joy, peace, long suffering, kindness, goodness, faithfulness, gentleness, self-control...*" Also imagine his wife doing the same thing. There will be harmony by default. You see, a good marriage is designed to be a by-product of the reality of the new covenant. Again, the overall message of this book is: each person in the marriage shouldn't focus on making the marriage work, but on Christ and His finished work of grace. If every couple will follow through with those 34 grace focused, Christ-centered pieces of advice discussed in this book for a month, they will only end up divorcing certain toxins in their marriage in order to remarry the brand new person their spouses are becoming.

However, the type of divorce I am referring to here is not the one that involves human beings in a marriage relationship but the one that involves issues. According to Wikipedia, the primary definition of divorce, also known as dissolution of marriage, is the process of terminating a marriage or marital union. The dictionary also refers to divorce as the legal dissolution of a marriage by a court or other competent body or authority. Typically, this type of divorce involves the persons or the couple in the marriage contract.

However, the dictionary also defines divorce as "to separate or dissociate (something) from something else." For instance, divorcing an issue from an individual. Essentially, divorce in this context can be defined as being able to separate a person from something. This second definition is what I referred to earlier. The couples are encouraged to focus on Christ and His finished work of grace on a daily basis. As they do this, the life-transforming nature of God in Christ through the power of the Holy Spirit helps them to separate or dissociate themselves from harmful dispositions that could negatively impact their marriage. Living a responsible Christian life which is a product of God's grace found in Christ is what enables us to divorce ourselves from terrible habits. As we get transformed into the image of Christ daily, old habits drop and we become new daily. This is what Paul the apostle calls renewing the mind (Romans 12:1-2). Imagine a man going through this type of transformation and the wife is going through the same experience in Christ. There will be a divorce of bad toxins while they are getting remarried to the new persons their partners are becoming.

For majority of the people it will not happen in one month. In fact, you are advised not to read through it in a hurry. Read a chapter a day, for a month including memorizing the Scriptures and praying the prayer focus for each day. This book is not a one-time read. It's a life manual. It is a continuous makeover process. The most beautiful women that I know wear their makeup every week. Some do it every day. In fact, some ladies would not even step out of their houses without their makeup on. If only we would embrace our relationship with Christ with this similar mindset. Makeover or transformations usually don't take place in seconds. They take time. If couples read this book three times a year together and trust God's grace to practice the Godly lifestyles recommended, it is guaranteed that we will have more joyful, fulfilling homes in our world.

Sam Ore
Maryland, U.S.A

POWER POINT 01

SIMPLIFY THE VISION OF YOUR MARRIAGE

SIMPLIFY THE VISION OF YOUR MARRIAGE

Simplifying the purpose of your marriage means avoiding complicated and unrealistic expectations. An excellent marriage is the one that is always focused on God's original purpose. Marriage is not man's idea but God's vision to explain the depth of the Trinitarian shared life with us. This shared life between God the Father, Jesus, and the Holy Spirit is characterized by absolute love, joy, peace, and harmony. We cannot fully enjoy our marriage to the fullest except we understand where it is coming from. Any attempt to enjoy anything in life outside of this revelation can at best be mechanical and frustrating.

Therefore, we must all begin the journey from our personal relationship with the Triune God followed by a great understanding of His vision for us as individuals. It was the volume of the work assigned to Adam that was responsible for the physical creation of Eve to help him. A great marriage therefore is in this order:

1. Personal relationship with God
2. Understanding your life's purpose
3. Social companionship
4. Emotional companionship
5. Sexual companionship
6. Pro-creation

A good grasp of number one above invariably will lead to the others by default. It is therefore imperative that couples don't lose focus of God's vision for the marriage. It is not just about them even though they should enjoy it to the fullest. The Author and Creator of marriage is far smarter and He is not tired of helping.

SCRIPTURE OF THE DAY

Habakkuk 2:1-4

"I will stand upon my watch, and set me upon the tower, and will watch to see what he will say unto me, and what I shall answer when I am reproved. ²And the Lord answered me, and said, Write the vision, and make it plain upon tables, that he may run that readeth it. ³For the vision is yet for an appointed time, but at the end it shall speak, and not lie: though it tarry, wait for it; because it will surely come, it will not tarry. ⁴Behold, his soul which is lifted up is not upright in him: but the just shall live by his faith." (KJV)

"I will climb up to my watchtower and stand at my guardpost. There I will wait to see what the Lord says and how he[a] will answer my complaint. ²Then the Lord said to me, "Write my answer plainly on tablets, so that a runner can carry the correct message to others. ³This vision is for a future time. It describes the end, and it will be fulfilled. If it seems slow in coming, wait patiently, for it will surely take

place. It will not be delayed. ⁴ *"Look at the proud! They trust in themselves, and their lives are crooked. But the righteous will live by their faithfulness to God."* (NLT)

Prayer focus for the Day

Lord, I receive clarity of Your vision for my family. I refuse to be disobedient to the vision in Jesus' name

DELETE TRADITIONS AND VAIN PHILOSOPHIES

It has been observed that when a lie is told repeatedly over a long period of time, it inevitably looks like the truth until it is challenged. Jesus Christ warns against vain traditions of men because they make God's word ineffective (Mark 7:13)

Paul the Apostle also encourages us to stay away from vain philosophies. (Colossian 2:8) Some of them look innocent on the surface but a closer look at them will reveal a distortion of the truth of God's word. Here are a few examples of innocent, distorted traditions of men either coined from individuals' experiences or outright misunderstanding of context of scriptures:

1) *Meet my better half.* When a person introduces his or her spouse as the better half, it is a harmless way of interpreting the spiritual equation of a man and a woman becoming one. The logic here is that only half plus half can become one. However, God's original intent was for a man that is whole to marry a woman that is also whole. Two whole, secured people in Christ can become one in the spirit as they focus on Christ without destroying their unique identities. God did not bring half Eve to half Adam.

2) *Don't give a woman an inch, if you do, she will go twelve miles.* A family member actually advised me with

those words a few days to our wedding. Even though I didn't allow it to sink but honestly, the words almost affected me at the beginning of our marriage each time my wife had a different opinion from mine. I had to intentionally delete it from my spiritual tabula rasa (blank state).

3) *Marriage is a necessary evil.* Why would anyone want to deliberately enter into something evil? We always should go back to the Creator's original vision for marriage. Did God really mean evil for Adam when He brought Eve to help him? If that were true, then God did Adam a lot of evil but we know God's core nature is love. Calling marriage a necessary evil is an invention of man. Delete it.

4) *"Every man must be married before he dies. No man should go unpunished."* This is funny but it is a vain philosophy.

5) *I love being married. It feels so great to find that one person you want to annoy for the rest of your life.* There is a story of a young boy who asked his Dad, "…Dad, how much does it cost to be married?" "My son, I don't know exactly because I am still paying". Replied his father sarcastically. Some of these expressions are borne out of personal frustrations of individuals but their stories don't have to become our own realities. God's revelation of truth is final. And Jesus Christ said "…I am the Way, the Truth, and the Life…" (John 14:6).

SCRIPTURE OF THE DAY
John 8:32

"And ye shall know the truth, and the truth shall make you free." (KJV)

"And you will know the truth, and the truth will set you free." (NLT)

"Then you will experience for yourselves the truth, and the truth will free you." (MSG)

Prayer focus for the Day

Heavenly Father, let the truth of the revelation of Christ and His finished work of grace delete every lie of the enemy in my life in Jesus' name.

GROW IN YOUR LOVE WALK

Believe God for more grace to grow in your love walk with God. God's love for you doesn't grow. It is perfect and final. It is complete and absolute. But your knowledge of Christ and what He accomplished is what makes you grow in grace and your love for Him. When you grow in grace, your love for your spouse also grows from ephemeral, transient things to something inexplicably deeper. Your love for your spouse starts growing from tangible to intangible.

At the beginning of your relationship, you can explain the reason why you love your spouse but as you grow in Christ, human explanation and reasons begin to fade away. At this point, the conditions begin to disappear. You don't say things like "I love you <u>whenever,</u>" "I love you <u>if,</u>" I love you <u>because,</u>" "I love you <u>only,</u>" "I love you <u>as long,</u>" or "I love you <u>anytime</u> you…" This is one of the reasons for crisis in marriages because the <u>ifs, when,</u> and <u>because</u> are subject to changes. Anytime there is a reason, it creates conditions and conditions create pressures for the other person. If you marry a man because of his six packs, he lives in pressure for the rest of his life to keep them. If you marry a woman because of her smooth skin, she becomes depressed when wrinkles are showing up later in life. When a lady marries a guy because of his money, he is put under pressure of making money till he dies. If a guy marries a lady just only to have children, she becomes bitter and insecure if she can't have children. This is one of the reasons for adultery in marriages. Confused couples start looking for other people who have the things their spouses don't have. People are no longer married to real people in their spouses. They are married to illusions and vain fantasies.

God wants us to get to a point when we love our spouses without a reason. Receive grace for this supernatural love in Jesus' mighty name.

SCRIPTURE OF THE DAY
Romans 8:37-39

"Nay, in all these things we are more than conquerors through him that loved us. For I am persuaded, that neither death, nor life, nor angels, nor principalities, nor powers, nor things present, nor things to come, Nor height, nor depth, nor any other creature, shall be able to separate us from the love of God, which is in Christ Jesus our Lord." (KJV)

"No, despite all these things, overwhelming victory is ours through Christ, who loved us. And I am convinced that nothing can ever separate us from God's love. Neither death nor life, neither angels nor demons,[a] neither our fears for today nor our worries about tomorrow—not even the powers of hell can separate us from God's love. No power in the sky above or in the earth below—indeed,

nothing in all creation will ever be able to separate us from the love of God that is revealed in Christ Jesus our Lord." (NLT)

"None of this fazes us because Jesus loves us. I'm absolutely convinced that nothing—nothing living or dead, angelic or demonic, today or tomorrow, high or low, thinkable or unthinkable—absolutely nothing can get between us and God's love because of the way that Jesus our Master has embraced us." (MSG)

Prayer focus for the Day

Dear heavenly Father, I do not have the capacity to truly love unconditionally until I have first embraced your unconditional love for myself. Since I cannot give what I don't have, I receive your overwhelming love today in Jesus' mighty name.

POWER POINT 04

CHOOSE YOUR CHURCH/ AFFILIATION WISELY

CHOOSE YOUR CHURCH/ AFFILIATION WISELY

It is imperative to stay connected to the same local church that is Jesus centered. There are many "good churches" but not many are Jesus Christ focused these days. This book is about a Christ-centered marriage. Therefore, it should never be about wanting a marriage to work but more about growing in Christ. Researches have shown that most couples that attend a living church together weekly have a better chance of success than couples who don't. It's even better when you both serve at the same local church. Unity and oneness on this point cannot be ignored. For instance, if your spouse is a member of a church that fundamentally teaches the doctrine of an angry, frustrated God who is always in a bad mood until He kills people but you are a committed member of a church that teaches that God's love for mankind is so deep and unconditional that He had to send His only Son to express that, there could be a major issue that will surface in other areas frequently. This is because the two of you are being influenced in different directions theologically. Read my book **"This Gospel Revelation:** Unveiling Jesus And The Coming Glory" for more explanation.

SCRIPTURE OF THE DAY

Amos 3:3

"Can two walk together, except they be agreed?" (KJV)

"Can two people walk together without agreeing on the direction?" (NLT)

"Do two people walk hand in hand if they aren't going to the same place?" (MSG)

Proverbs 13:20

"He that walketh with wise men shall be wise: but a companion of fools shall be destroyed." (KJV)

"Walk with the wise and become wise; associate with fools and get in trouble." (NLT)

"Become wise by walking with the wise; hang out with fools and watch your life fall to pieces." (MSG)

Prayer focus for the Day

We stand together in unity of purpose and God's vision for our lives. We receive guidance to a local church that is Christ-centered in Jesus' mighty name.

UNDERSTAND YOUR SPOUSE'S DYNAMICS

One of the major causes of unresolved problems in most marriage relationships is the lack of understanding of the different dynamics of the male and female genders. The man and the woman are different in many ways regarding their psychological makeups. See below a few examples.

1) Men are logical thinkers and women are emotional feelers. While men think about mortgages, school fees, and other things they consider important, their wives are thinking about vacations, family movie nights, new clothes for the children, etc. because these things are more important to them. Therefore, husbands and wives need to believe God for grace to switch roles mentally so they can understand their spouses and walk in unity.

2) When discussing the vision for the future, men are excited, but the women want to know how to get there. However, when it comes to material blessings such as houses, furniture, bags, shoes, shopping, etc., women are excited but the men want to know how to get there.

3) The number one need of a man is respect (because of his God-given ego), not sex. There is no record that Samson had sex with Delilah. She simply massaged

his ego and he fell flat. Ephesians 5:22-23 says, "For wives, this means submit to your husbands as to the Lord. For a husband is the head of his wife as Christ is the head of the church. He is the Savior of his body, the church." (NLT). The number one need of a woman is not sex but affection. That's why Ephesians 5:25 says "For husbands, this means love your wives, just as Christ loved the church. He gave up his life for her." (NLT).

4) Men are givers while women are receivers. They are wired like that genetically. That is why responsible men are depressed and angry when they cannot pay the bills and take care of their families. Men are the seed sowers while women are the incubators. Because women expand just about anything and everything you give them, men should be careful about what they are sowing into their lives.

While speaking in a conference a few years ago, I advised the men with these words. When you give your wife a sperm, she will give you a baby or babies as the case may be. Give her a word, expect a phrase. Give her a phrase and she will give you a sentence. Give her a sentence, and reap a paragraph. Give your wife a paragraph and she will give you a page. Give her a page and expect a chapter. Give her a chapter and she will turn it into a book. Give her a book and she will you a library. Give her a library and expect a harvest of a world full of books everywhere.

Women are wonderful creatures. Let the men treat them with respect by being careful of what we sow into their lives.

SCRIPTURE OF THE DAY
Ephesians 5:20-32

"And give thanks for everything to God the Father in the name of our Lord Jesus Christ.

[21] And further, submit to one another out of reverence for Christ.

[22] For wives, this means submit to your husbands as to the Lord. [23] For a husband is the head of his wife as Christ is the head of the church. He is the Savior of his body, the church. [24] As the church submits to Christ, so you wives should submit to your husbands in everything.

[25] For husbands, this means love your wives, just as Christ loved the church. He gave up his life for her [26] to make her holy and clean, washed by the cleansing of God's word. [27] He did this to present her to himself as a glorious church without a spot or wrinkle or any other blemish. Instead, she will be holy and without fault. [28] In the same way, husbands ought to love their wives as they love their own bodies. For a man who loves his wife actually shows love for himself. [29] No one hates his own body but feeds and cares for it, just as Christ cares for the church. [30] And we are members of his body.

[31] As the Scriptures say, "A man leaves his father and mother and is joined to his wife, and the two are united into one."[32] This is a great mystery, but it is an illustration of the way Christ and the church are one." (NLT)

Prayer focus for the Day

Dear heavenly Father, I receive supernatural wisdom today to respond to the needs of my spouse in a way that is Godly and respectful as I focus on Christ and His finished work of grace in Jesus' name.

PAY ATTENTION TO TRIANGULATION

One of the challenges in any marriage is the negative third party influence. It is also known as triangulation. It is a term used as manipulation method where one person will not communicate directly with another person instead use a third person to relay communication to the second thus forming a triangle. Triangulation is not limited to actual persons, it could also be opinions, idosyncracracies, habits, etc that are transferred from external sources to your marriage. For instance, trying to run your family the way your parents run theirs is an example of triangulation. Triangulation is not inherently evil as long as values are communicated. Basically, a negative triangle is created when one spouse brings in a third party for an unhealthy reason. For instance, a husband (person A) goes to a friend (person C) for something instead of going to his wife (person B) thereby creating a conflict in the process.

Create reasonable boundaries for friends, in-laws, and associates. It is a known fact that most crises in marriages are caused or intensified by either friends or family members. These friends and families are not all bad people but sometimes their influence can be negative if we don't create reasonable boundaries.

We should treat our in-laws, families, and friends with

respect. We should also bless them with whatever we can afford per time in love because they are still part of our lives but the point is we can't take our spouses to the altar of sacrifice for our relatives. Trust God for grace and wisdom to maintain a reasonable balance.

SCRIPTURE OF THE DAY
Matthew 19:5-6

"And said, For this cause shall a man leave father and mother, and shall cleave to his wife: and they twain shall be one flesh? Wherefore they are no more twain, but one flesh. What therefore God hath joined together, let not man put asunder." (KJV)

"And he said, "'This explains why a man leaves his father and mother and is joined to his wife, and the two are united into one.' Since they are no longer two but one, let no one split apart what God has joined together." (NLT)

"He answered, "Haven't you read in your Bible that the Creator originally made man and woman for each other, male and female? And because of this, a man leaves father and mother and is firmly bonded to his wife, becoming one flesh—no longer two bodies but one. Because God created this organic union of the two sexes, no one should desecrate his art by cutting them apart." (Matthew 19:4-6, MSG)

Prayer focus for the Day

Heavenly Father, I receive
supernatural wisdom to walk in love with
everybody connected to my family
in Jesus' name.

UNDERSTANDING DIFFERENT STAGES OF MARRIAGE

UNDERSTANDING DIFFERENT STAGES OF MARRIAGE

Have you ever taken a rollercoaster ride before? Well, marriage can be described as a rollercoaster experience. I believe God uses these different experiences as catalysts for our growth as individuals and as couples. These 5 stages are explained below.

1. *The romance stage/ head over heels love experience.* This is also called the fantasy moment. It is a stage where both of you are "drunk" with love. A season where you can hardly have enough of each other as time quickly flies away. Couples sacrifice just about anything for their partners here. It is usually from dating to honeymoon for about 6 months to 2 years. It varies. The romance stage is also called the passion stage. This is the stage where you hear romantic words from men like "My most brilliant achievement was my ability to be able to persuade my wife to marry me." And the wife will respond, "Honey, I love you to pieces." Then they move into the next phase.

2. *From the romance phase, couples tend to transition into disappointment/disillusion stage.* At this point, you start realizing that your partner is not as impeccable as you thought, you start seeing each other's faults and shortcomings. The utopia vision of the happy

married life starts fading away. Depending on the level and the intensity of their romance, most couples will still have extra in their tank to carry them through this stage. That's why it is important to make enough deposit during the romance stage because you will need to make. This stage is also known as the realization stage.

3. *The third phase is called the power struggle stage or the distress stage.* This is the time when things get more complicated especially if the disillusion stage is not properly managed. Withdrawal symptoms set in. Couples become estranged. Deep resentments and bitterness begin to build up. This is where most couples get stuck and they start thinking of divorce. It is also known as the rebellion stage.

4. *The stability or cooperation stage.* If a couple can make it to this point, chances are that they have become more matured. This stage is also known as reconciliation phase. They start feeling more connected. They resolve conflict with respect and understanding. In some instances, they start growing in their unique purpose and personal goals. Although, the danger here is that couples may drift apart at this stage if care is not taken.

5. *The reunion stage, also known as the transformation phase.* This is the time when couples have decided to accept each other for who they are. Nobody is trying to

change the other person. It's not as if everything is perfect, but the couples have resolved to stick together no matter what. The couples are no longer together because they need each other, but because they choose to stay married regardless of the challenges. Most couples who make it to this phase will remain married to the end of times. This phase is also called the completion stage. It is highly imperative to remember that a laser focus on Christ and His finished work of grace is your only anchor from the first phase to the last one. Again, God's grace is the only hope for true Christian marriage. The honest truth is that a lot of couples who opt out for divorce by refusing to go all the way to the completion phase have only denied themselves the opportunity to grow. This is not being judgmental. The good news is that if God ever gives them another opportunity, they would have been armed with this truth. The completion stage is when the couple goes through the complete cycle of marriage. From being only two people at the beginning before the children come. And then the children leave to start their own families, after which the couple becomes empty nesters and the two of them remain as they were at the beginning of their love journey except that they are now more matured and their love for each other has grown deeper.

Receive grace to transition all the way to completion stage in Jesus' mighty name.

SCRIPTURE OF THE DAY
I Corinthians 13:4-7

"Charity suffereth long, and is kind; charity envieth not; charity vaunteth not itself, is not puffed up, [5] Doth not behave itself unseemly, seeketh not her own, is not easily provoked, thinketh no evil; [6] Rejoiceth not in iniquity, but rejoiceth in the truth; [7] Beareth all things, believeth all things, hopeth all things, endureth all things." (KJV)

"Love is patient and kind. Love is not jealous or boastful or proud [5] or rude. It does not demand its own way. It is not irritable, and it keeps no record of being wronged. [6] It does not rejoice about injustice but rejoices whenever the truth wins out. [7] Love never gives up, never loses faith, is always hopeful, and endures through every circumstance." (NLT)

"Love never gives up. Love cares more for others than for self. Love doesn't want what it doesn't have. Love doesn't strut, Doesn't have a swelled head, Doesn't force itself on others, Isn't always "me first," Doesn't fly off the handle, Doesn't keep score of the sins of others, Doesn't revel when others grovel, Takes pleasure in the flowering of truth, Puts up with anything, Trusts God always, Always looks

*for the b*est, Never looks back, But keeps going to the end." (MSG)

Prayer focus for the Day

Heavenly Father, I receive supernatural understanding today to grow into maturity during these different stages of my marriage in Jesus' name.

POWER POINT
08

SACRIFICIAL LOVE: HUSBANDS

SACRIFICIAL LOVE: HUSBANDS

Most men think they truly love their wives until they read Ephesians 5:22 in context. The love here is an encapsulation of the different types of love I described in my book "TOWARDS A PURPOSEFUL MARRIAGE."

Platonic - innocent, no strings attached pure love

Erotic - sensual type with a sexual undertone

Felial love - between family

Conjugal - God's perfect love between husband and wife

Agape – God's perfect love

The honest truth is that no man can adequately walk in all these types of love consistently without the grace of God. Someone said: if not for marriage, most men will go through life thinking they are perfect. That's why Ephesians chapter 5 (The Marna Epistle) begins with the focus on Christ our only hope.

This all-encompassing love is so sacrificial that the man should be willing to "die" - give up anything for the sake of his wife. These include his destructive ego, comfort, family, opinion, and his material possessions. Ironically, when a husband does this for his wife, a grace filled wife will willingly submit. The husband should lead with dignity and respect. When the husband carries out his God-given responsibility, his wife responds willingly. But when the husband demands, his wife reacts instead of responding. When her husband commits, she submits. When her husband gives, she responds. Both husband and wife should never use love and submission as tools for manipulation. A pastor was trying to practically illustrate his message on why women should not control their husbands asked that all the men who were being controlled by their wives move to the left side of the auditorium. All the men moved except one man. The pastor was so disappointed at the men. "…I am appalled by you weak men who allow your wives to tell you what to do…" Turning to the only man who did not move, the pastor was excited that at least he had one man in his church who refused to be controlled by his wife. "…My brother, so, why did you not move?" Asked the pastor. "My wife gave me a sign that I should not move." And that was the end of the service. That's why both husband and wife must never lose focus on Christ. That's where they draw their strength from. Receive strength today in Jesus Christ's name.

SCRIPTURE OF THE DAY

Ephesians 5:25-27

"Husbands, love your wives, even as Christ also loved the church, and gave himself for it; That he might sanctify and cleanse it with the washing of water by the word, That he might present it to himself a glorious church, not having spot, or wrinkle, or any such thing; but that it should be holy and without blemish." (KJV)

"For husbands, this means love your wives, just as Christ loved the church. He gave up his life for her to make her holy and clean, washed by the cleansing of God's word. He did this to present her to himself as a glorious church without a spot or wrinkle or any other blemish. Instead, she will be holy and without fault." (NLT)

"Husbands, go all out in your love for your wives, exactly as Christ did for the church—a love marked by giving, not getting. Christ's love makes the church whole. His words evoke her beauty. Everything he does and says is designed to bring the best out of her, dressing her in dazzling white silk, radiant with holiness. And that is how husbands ought to love their wives. They're really doing themselves a favor—since they're already "one" in marriage." (MSG)

Prayer focus for the Day

Dear Lord Jesus, I focus on your love for me for the strength to love my wife as you love me in Jesus' mighty name.

WILLING SUBMISSION: WIVES

WILLING SUBMISSION: WIVES

This is a big one: First of all, submission is not subjugation. It is not slavery. Submission is not punishment.

Submission has nothing to do with suppressing or destroying your wife's will, spirit, desires, happiness, intellect, gifts, aspiration, personality, or vision. She is not a robot or a zombie. Submission is a willing act of service as a result of revelation of grace. To submit means to intentionally and willingly recognize and affirm the God-given vision and responsibility of the husband. Real biblical submission is not coercive or forcefully demanded in an authoritative manner. A true grace based submission is that of position and role rather than persuasion. The identity and uniqueness of the woman is not destroyed in the name of submission. Ironically, a wife that truly submits to her husband in the proper context described above automatically attracts a deeper, corresponding affection from a Godly husband. The key is: loving your wife the way Jesus loves the church and submitting to your husband like the way the church does to Jesus cannot be achieved without God's grace. Receive wisdom to willingly submit to your husband today through the eye of grace in the name of Jesus Christ.

SCRIPTURE OF THE DAY
Ephesians 5:21-24

"Giving thanks always for all things unto God and the Father in the name of our Lord Jesus Christ; Submitting yourselves one to another in the fear of God. Wives, submit yourselves unto your own husbands, as unto the Lord. For the husband is the head of the wife, even as Christ is the head of the church: and he is the saviour of the body. Therefore as the church is subject unto Christ, so let the wives be to their own husbands in every thing." (KJV)

"And give thanks for everything to God the Father in the name of our Lord Jesus Christ. And further, submit to one another out of reverence for Christ. For wives, this means submit to your husbands as to the Lord. 23 For a husband is the head of his wife as Christ is the head of the church. He is the Savior of his body, the church. As the church submits to Christ, so you wives should submit to your husbands in everything." (NLT)

"Out of respect for Christ, be courteously reverent to one another. Wives, understand and support your husbands in ways that show your support for Christ. The husband provides leadership to his wife the way Christ does to

his church, not by domineering but by cherishing. So just as the church submits to Christ as he exercises such leadership, wives should likewise submit to their husbands." (MSG)

Prayer focus for the Day

Father, I receive grace, wisdom, and strength to submit to my husband in the Spirit of wholeness and a personal revelation of Christ in Jesus' name.

SAY NO TO COMPARISON

One of the honest, brutal truths about true definition of foolishness according to the Scripture is comparison. II Corinthians 10:12 says, "For we dare not class ourselves or compare ourselves with those who commend themselves. But they, measuring themselves by themselves, and comparing themselves among themselves, are not wise." (NKJV). Never compare yourself or your spouse with anyone. I know it is easier said than done. God's word says those who do this are not wise. This is because if you compare your family with those you think you are better off, pride could set in. On the other hand, if you compare yourself with those you think are better than you, you can be depressed or become jealous.

You can show the compassion of Jesus to those who are having a rough time while you believe God for the same grace that is helping those you admire their marriage. Either way, you are unique, different, and special where you are now not-withstanding.

What a lot of couples don't realize is that, the proverbial greener grass on the other side applies to marriage too. Most marital challenges are similar. A frustrated lady posted a classified ad in the newspaper with the caption "Husband wanted." Within four days, she received over five hundred letters saying the same thing "you can have mine." The moral of this story is that do not let circumstances exaggerate your challenges by thinking that you are the only one going through all the problems in this world. I Corinthians 10:13 says, "The temptations in your life are no different from what others experience. And God is faithful. He will not allow the temptation to be more than you stand. When you are tempted, He will show you a way out so that you can endure." (NLT).

SCRIPTURE OF THE DAY
II Corinthians 10:12

"For we dare not make ourselves of the number, or compare ourselves with some that commend themselves: but they measuring themselves by themselves, and comparing themselves among themselves, are not wise." (KJV)

"Oh, don't worry; we wouldn't dare say that we are as wonderful as these other men who tell you how important they are! But they are only comparing themselves with each other, using themselves as the standard of measurement. How ignorant!" (NLT)

"We're not, understand, putting ourselves in a league with those who boast that they're our superiors. We wouldn't dare do that. But in all this comparing and grading and competing, they quite miss the point." (MSG)

Prayer focus for the Day

Heavenly Father, we thank you for
the uniqueness of our marriage.
We trust you for more grace
in Jesus' name.

MARRIAGE PHYSICAL CHECKUP

It's amazing how we take time to do yearly physical for our health but we ignore the health of our marriage. Just like our physical health, the overall health of your marriage depends on what you are feeding it with, the amount of rest you have and your fitness exercise level. Health therapists advise that for a person to be healthy, he needs to eat healthy foods, take adequate rest and exercise. So it is with the health of your marriage. Healthy foods (teachings and resources you are being fed with regularly) are very crucial.

What about adequate rest? How much of Jesus and His grace are you allowing in your marriage?

Matthew 11:28-30 (MSG) states, "Are you tired? Worn out? Burned out on religion? Come to me. Get away with me and you'll recover your life. I'll show you how to take a real rest. Walk with me and work with me—watch how I do it. Learn the unforced rhythms of grace. I won't lay anything heavy or ill-fitting on you. Keep company with me and you'll learn to live freely and lightly."

Also, to stay healthy, people are advised to go for physical examination with a licensed, trusted physician yearly or even bi-annually depending on your age bracket. People's physical health and fitness level will fall into at least one of these categories mentioned below. And we can use this analysis for the health of our marriage too.

1. Is your marriage healthy?
2. Is your marriage sick with certain symptoms?
3. Is your marriage in a terminal stage?
4. Is your marriage in a coma?
5. Is your marriage dead?

Notice the sequence above. From being healthy to symptomatic problems all the way to a dead marriage. This means that marriages don't just die in one day, it takes time. Pay attention to the stages before the final divorce. Divorces don't just happen. One of the beautiful things about symptoms is that they can be paradoxical. They can be painful but they can be good at the same time. The pain that accompanies a symptom can help to quickly diagnose a tragic health issue for immediate treatment. The fact that a couple in any marriage can still feel pain is an indication that the marriage is still alive. When a husband or a wife does not care anymore regardless of the level of pain, then the marriage is dead.

The good news is that Jesus Christ can treat any of these cases including raising a dead one. By God's grace my wife and I have seen divorces upturned many times through the grace of God when troubled couples are counseled to refocus on Christ and His finished work of grace.

Again, it can be practically frustrating when the main objective is to make the marriage work instead of the couple just believing God for more grace through the knowledge of the Lord Jesus Christ.

I speak health into your marriage today in Jesus' mighty name.

SCRIPTURE OF THE DAY
Proverbs 4:20-23

"My son, attend to my words; incline thine ear unto my sayings. Let them not depart from thine eyes; keep them in the midst of thine heart. For they are life unto those that find them, and health to all their flesh. Keep thy heart with all diligence; for out of it are the issues of life." (KJV)

"My child, pay attention to what I say. Listen carefully to my words. Don't lose sight of them. Let them penetrate deep into your heart, for they bring life to those who find them, and healing to their whole body. Guard your heart above all else, for it determines the course of your life." (NLT)

"Dear friend, listen well to my words; tune your ears to my voice. Keep my message in plain view at all times. Concentrate! Learn it by heart! Those who discover these words live, really live; body and soul, they're bursting with health. **Keep vigilant watch over your heart; that's where life starts."** *(MSG)*

Prayer focus for the Day

Dear Lord, I declare healing and sound health over my marriage in Jesus' name.

APPRECIATE YOUR SPOUSE

Appreciate each other and be grateful to God. Start everyday with an appreciative heart and a thanksgiving heart for God's grace on your spouse. Don't always feel entitled. A sense of entitlement will always produce an ungrateful heart, and it has ruined many marriages.

Several years ago, my wife and I were on vacation. While waiting for our luggage to arrive, I noticed her teary eyes. "Are you okay?" I asked. With a soft voice, she whispered, "...I thank God for your life. Where would I be if not for you?" I quickly responded, "It's actually the other way around. I am the blessed man with a wife like you."

Learn to appreciate your spouse no matter what you may be going through. Appreciation creates the desire to be better in any normal human being and negative criticism leads to rebellion and bitterness. Think deeply and you will always find something positive to say about your spouse.

A man once said to his wife: I looked into my wallet and it was empty. I looked through all my pockets and they were empty. Then I looked into my heart and I found you and only then I figured out how rich I was. What a way to show appreciation with words.

Being appreciative of your spouse creates an atmosphere of peace. Do it today and do it now.

SCRIPTURE OF THE DAY
I Corinthians 1:4

"I thank my God always on your behalf, for the grace of God which is given you by Jesus Christ" (KJV)

"I always thank my God for you and for the gracious gifts he has given you, now that you belong to Christ Jesus" (NLT)

"Every time I think of you—and I think of you often!—I thank God for your lives of free and

Prayer focus for the Day

Heavenly Father, I am grateful for the
different manifestations of your
goodness on my spouse
in Jesus' name.

UNDERSTANDING THE SEASONS OF MARRIAGE

Every marriage, like nature, will go through different seasons. The natural cyclical seasons of life are spring, summer, fall, and winter.

We can take advantage of the different experiences during these seasons to grow in our walk with God which will invariably help our marriage. "As expected, most marriages begin in Spring and evolve into Summer…" says Dr. Gary Chapman. Spring is arguably the best season of most marriages. There is a feeling of excitement, enthusiasm, and anticipation of good things to come. It is the season of lovey dovey euphoria.

It even gets better and more passionate in summer. The summer season is warm with romance, positive attitude and everything is looking beautiful. There is this feeling of accomplishment, satisfaction, and connection. Unfortunately, just like no season is permanent in nature, the marital summer gives way to the fall. A season where a marriage may look fine on the outside but things may be falling apart on the inside. And the couples start feeling like the honeymoon is over.

The fall season is when symptomatic problems affecting the health of the marriage start showing up. Please study the chapter on the health of your marriage again.

From fall, every marriage moves into the winter season. This is when marriages go through cold period. The passion is waning down. Energy is low and couples are becoming withdrawn. If they didn't handle the fall season very well, there is a carryover of the issues into the winter except that these problems may have snowballed into resentment, bitterness, and major crisis. Winter season is when what attracted you to your spouse at the beginning is now irritating you and vice-versa.

One of the things Debby loved about me when we first met, according to her, was my ability to communicate with charisma and she would not be bored. In fact, on many occasions during our courtship, she would just be staring at me with a smile. One day I asked her, "Why were you looking at me like that when I was talking to my friend?" Her gracious, romantic answer was "I am just thanking God for giving me an intelligent man like you."

Ironically, during certain seasons of winter in our marriage, she does not want me to talk at all. In fact, she occasionally teases me that I preach too long. On the other hand, her quiet demeanor that attracted me to her almost irritated me at a certain season of our winter. I felt she was too quiet for a preacher's wife.

For some couples, they get attracted by the dress sense of their spouse which will later become an irritation. It's important to note at this point that these seasons unlike the natural ones do not follow a particular order during the year. In fact, you may experience them multiple times within a week or a month.

The most important thing to be aware of is to be pro-active and get ready to face the challenges especially the fall and winter seasons. This is the time to speak more hope and grace-filled words to each other. You can use the harshness and the frustration of the winter season to grow in Christ and His finished work of grace instead of tearing down each other (Ephesians 4:29). It won't be long when the summer sun will shine on you again. May God's grace keep you in Jesus' name.

SCRIPTURE OF THE DAY
Genesis 8:22

"While the earth remaineth, seedtime and harvest, and cold and heat, and summer and winter, and day and night shall not cease." (KJV)

"As long as the earth remains, there will be planting and harvest, cold and heat, summer and winter, day and night." (NLT)

"For as long as Earth lasts, planting and harvest, cold and heat, Summer and winter, day and night will never stop." (MSG)

Prayer focus for the Day

Dear Heavenly Father, I receive grace to turn every season into heaven on Earth for my family in Jesus' mighty name.

POWER POINT 14

LEARN TO RELAX TOGETHER

LEARN TO RELAX TOGETER

Endeavor not to take life seriously. Have fun. Relax with nature such as seas, fresh air, beaches, etc. Spending time together in these types of natural environments can be therapeutic. Studies show that calm, serene tranquil environments can activate our creative imaginations. Marriage is not meant to be laborious.

Marriage should be enjoyed. Ecclesiastes 9:9 says, *"Live happily with the woman you love through all the meaningless days of life that God has given you under the sun. The wife God gives you is your reward for all your earthly toil."* (NLT).

Choose your social life intentionally and in the Spirit. Take time to enjoy weddings, birthday parties, etc. A true life of fulfillment cannot just be about work and no play. Even our Lord Jesus Christ Himself had a vibrant, social life during His earthly ministry. For instance, He attended the wedding reception at the marriage in Canaan of Galilee. It is not a sin to have fun and enjoy life together especially when you have worked hard

SCRIPTURE OF THE DAY
John 2:1-11

"The next day there was a wedding celebration in the village of Cana in Galilee.

Jesus' mother was there, and Jesus and his disciples were also invited to the celebration. The wine supply ran out during the festivities, so Jesus' mother told him, "They have no more wine."

"Dear woman, that's not our problem," Jesus replied. "My time has not yet come."

But his mother told the servants, "Do whatever he tells you."

Standing nearby were six stone water jars, used for Jewish ceremonial washing. Each could hold twenty to thirty gallons.

Jesus told the servants, "Fill the jars with water." When the jars had been filled, he said, "Now dip some out, and take it to the master of ceremonies." So the servants followed his instructions. When the master of ceremonies tasted the water that was now wine, not knowing where it had come from (though, of course, the servants knew), he called the bridegroom over. "A host always serves the best wine first," he said. "Then, when everyone has had a lot to drink, he brings out the less expensive wine. But you have kept the best until now!" This miraculous sign at Cana in Galilee was the first time Jesus revealed his glory. And his disciples believed in him."
(NLT)

Prayer focus for the Day

Heavenly Father, I receive a creative and relaxed mind to help my spouse today in Jesus' name.

UNDERSTANDING A THREE-PRONG COMMUNICATION

UNDERSTANDING A THREE-PRONG COMMUNICATION

A three-prong, effective communication is one of the hopelines of a good marriage. Don't just hear your spouse, try to listen. There is a big difference between the two. These are the three prong components of good communication:

1. Ensure that people understand not only what you say, but also what you mean. Ensure that your spouse not only understands you, but also understands what your intents are.

2. Avoid ambiguities and offensive words.

3. Use the right tone. Developing these aspects of communication requires grace and skills. The language and the style used to communicate are very important.

When trying to communicate to each other, couples should endeavor to make sure that their voices, faces, and body languages agree with their words. For instance, wife asks "are you okay?" and husband yells out, "I am okay." Saying the right thing while yelling is not good communication. Your tone and body language must align with your desired intent. This is also called empathetic active listening. Pay attention to words that should never be used under any circumstances: They are "I regret marrying you," "you are a failure," "you are pathetic," "you are a fool," etc. A woman once said to her husband, "I regret marrying you. I should have married the devil." The husband responded, "If you had done that, you would have been arrested because marriage between relatives in this country is illegal." The implication is that his wife is a relative of the devil.

No matter how upset you are, your words should never destroy your spouse but rather build them up. Start speaking the right words at the right time today in Jesus' name.

SCRIPTURE OF THE DAY
Ephesians 4:29

"Let no corrupt communication proceed out of your mouth, but that which is good to the use of edifying, that it may minister grace unto the hearers." (KJV)

"Don't use foul or abusive language. Let everything you say be good and helpful, so that your words will be an encouragement to those who hear them." (NLT)

"Watch the way you talk. Let nothing foul or dirty come out of your mouth. Say only what helps, each word a gift." (MSG)

Prayer focus for the Day

Lord, help me to effectively communicate with my spouse today in a gracious manner in Jesus' mighty name.

LEARNING TO ADMIRE YOUR SPOUSE ALL OVER AGAIN

One of the greatest enemies of a fulfilling marriage is familiarity. You must intentionally contend with it. Admire your spouse's great attributes through the eyes of Christ. Constant negative criticism of your spouse is counter-productive. It will lead to rebellion. But when you focus on your spouse's great qualities just like Christ does for all of us, your spouse is edified. It is natural for the flesh to concentrate on the weaknesses of your spouse. Nobody needs faith to do that. It takes faith to do otherwise. You need faith to look away from the weaknesses. Faith in this context is not self-denial but a deliberate, intentional habit of concentrating on the positive side of your spouse. Philippians 4:8 says, *"And now, dear brothers and sisters, one final thing. Fix your thoughts on what is true, and honorable, and right, and pure, and lovely, and admirable. Think about things that are excellent and worthy of praise"* (NLT). A wise man once said: A great marriage is not when the perfect couple comes together. It is when an imperfect couple learns to enjoy their differences. The truth is that what makes a marriage more interesting is not how compatible you are but how you deal with your incompatibility. Receive grace in Jesus' name.

SCRIPTURE OF THE DAY
Romans 12:10

"Be kindly affectioned one to another with brotherly love; in honour preferring one

another" (KJV)

"Love each other with genuine affection, and take delight in honoring each other" (NLT)

"Love from the center of who you are; don't fake it. Run for dear life from evil; hold on for dear life to good. Be good friends who love deeply; practice playing second fiddle." (MSG)

Prayer focus for the Day

Lord, I receive grace to see my spouse the way You see him/her with the eyes of grace in Jesus mighty name.

UNDERSTANDING TRUE FORGIVENESS

As long as we remain in this terrestrial divide, we will always have differences. You should never forget that you and your spouse are still human with tendencies to make mistakes. It has been observed that nobody loses credibility for making mistakes but people lose credibility for not acknowledging and accepting responsibility for their mistakes. Learn to forgive and believe God for the grace to move on. Stop dwelling on past mistakes.

There is this story of a couple on a particular flight. The pilot announced "...ladies and gentlemen, there is a bad news. I just got disconnected from the control tower and one of the engines has shut down. I don't know exactly where we are. Please get ready to meet your maker." he concluded. In the middle of the pandemonium, a man looked at his wife "Sweetie, I have a confession to make." With tears in his eyes he said, "That lady I introduced to you as my business partner is actually my side chick. I have been fooling around with her for more than three years. Please forgive me." With tears in her eyes, the wife responded, "I am pleading for your forgiveness too because you are not the father of our seven children." Just as the couple cuddled themselves to meet their maker in peace, the announcement came from the intercom "Hello, ladies and gentlemen, I just reconnected back to the control tower and we are landing safely in about thirty minutes." "No, this plane must crash," yelled the man. Apparently, he didn't want to deal with the horror of living with an unfaithful wife and children that are not his own. But the reality is that they are both guilty.

The moral of this fictional story is that if we look closely and objectively, there will always be offenses in any relationship especially at the beginning. They become less frequent as both mature in God's grace. Believe God for abundant grace to forgive. After all, God's word says "love covers multitude of sins…" (I Peter 4:8).

Sometimes, the way certain things were terribly handled in the past may prevent the aggrieved party from opening up again. Receive grace and wisdom to have open discussions on important issues without fear or shame in Jesus Name.

SCRIPTURE OF THE DAY
Ephesians 4:32

"And be ye kind one to another, tenderhearted, forgiving one another, even as God for Christ's sake hath forgiven you." (KJV)

"Instead, be kind to each other, tenderhearted, forgiving one another, just as God through Christ has forgiven you." (NLT)

"Forgive one another as quickly and thoroughly as God in Christ forgave you." (MSG)

Prayer focus for the Day

Dear Lord, open my eyes of understanding to see the depth of Jesus' forgiveness and His love so that I can extend the same to my spouse in Jesus' mighty name.

POWER POINT 18

BE INTENTIONAL ABOUT FINANCIAL MATTERS

BE INTENTIONAL ABOUT FINANCIAL MATTERS

It is no longer a mystery that sex is no longer the number one cause of divorce but, other issues related to the general well-being of the family. The challenge is real and it can put a lot of burdens on the overall health of a family if not properly addressed. Be intentional about budgeting and financial planning. Bring in professionals and experts where necessary. Believe God for the grace to manage the resources He has committed into your hands by being good stewards before believing God for more. You have to be good managers first. Effective managers not only manage what they are given, they preserve and multiply resources. Receive miraculous wisdom for effective financial management today in Jesus' name.

According to a recent poll, the leading causes of divorce are listed in this order:

Lack of commitment – 75%

Infidelity – 59.6%

Frequent conflicts – 57.7%

Too early and immature marriages – 45.1%

Financial issues – 36.1%

Substance abuse – 34.6%

Domestic abuse – 23.5%

Health issues – 18.2%

Family interference – 17.3%

Lack or little pre-marital education – 13.3%

Interestingly, when the poll is narrowed to the church, money becomes the number one leading cause of stress in marriage or outright divorce. At this point, I must admit that I have not been personally responsible in teaching financial management. I seize this opportunity to apologize to everyone that has been mentored by me one way or another. Please forgive me. A lot of preachers, including me, have always emphasized the need to be generous, start a business, career improvements, etc. These are all great. And we have done well by God's grace on these fronts, but financial management is a missing puzzle that should not be ignored.

The truth is that we all make money decisions every single day. The odds that misunderstandings may go to another level when making those decisions with another person are higher. It is therefore imperative to stick to the old principle of financial intelligence regarding money: make all you can, give all you can, and save all you can.

SCRIPTURE OF THE DAY
Genesis 41:34-36

"Let Pharaoh do this, and let him appoint officers over the land, and take up the fifth part of the land of Egypt in the seven plenteous years. And let them gather all the food of those good years that come, and lay up corn under the hand

of Pharaoh, and let them keep food in the cities. And that food shall be for store to the land against the seven years of famine, which shall be in the land of Egypt; that the land perish not through the famine" (KJV)

"Then Pharaoh should appoint supervisors over the land and let them collect one-fifth of all the crops during the seven good years. Have them gather all the food produced in the good years that are just ahead and bring it to Pharaoh's storehouses. Store it away, and guard it so there will be food in the cities. That way there will be enough to eat when the seven years of famine come to the land of Egypt. Otherwise this famine will destroy the land." (NLT)

"So, Pharaoh needs to look for a wise and experienced man and put him in charge of the country. Then Pharaoh needs to appoint managers throughout the country of Egypt to organize it during the years of plenty. Their job will be to collect all the food produced in the good years ahead and stockpile the grain under Pharaoh's authority, storing it in the towns for food. This grain will be held back to be used later during the seven years of famine that are coming on Egypt. This way the country won't be devastated by the famine." (Genesis 41: 33-36, MSG)

Ecclesiastes 11:2

"Give a portion to seven, and also to eight; for thou knowest not what evil shall be upon the earth." (KJV)

"But divide your investments among many places, for you do not know what risks might lie ahead." (NLT)

"Don't hoard your goods; spread them around. Be a blessing to others. This could be your last night." (MSG)

Prayer focus for the Day

Dear Lord, I receive divine creativity to manage your resources and to multiply them in Jesus' name.

POWER POINT 19

LEARN TO SPEAK YOUR SPOUSE'S LANGUAGE

LEARN TO SPEAK YOUR SPOUSE'S LANGUAGE

Words are powerful. They can edify or destroy. A lot of marriages have been ruined because of inappropriate languages. Speak your spouse's love language. Do not assume you understand your spouse's love language. Assumption is a robber of meaningful conversation. Dr. Gary Chapman discusses them excellently in his book THE 5 LOVE LANGUAGES.

Words of affirmation.

Acts of service.

Receiving gifts.

Quality time.

Physical touch.

The interesting thing is that I Corinthians 13 captures all of these love languages. Simply embracing the love of God through Christ and sharing the same with people around you including your spouse captures the five love languages. Again, when the focus is Christ and His finished work of grace, a joyful marriage is one of the benefits. When we grow in grace, we will affirm, serve, give gifts, invest quality time with our love ones, and show physical affection by touching. All these physical love languages will be demonstrated by default as products of the work of grace.

SCRIPTURE OF THE DAY
Galatians 5:22-23

"But the fruit of the Spirit is love, joy, peace, long-suffering, gentleness, goodness, faith,

Meekness, temperance: against such there is no law." (KJV)

"But the Holy Spirit produces this kind of fruit in our lives: love, joy, peace, patience, kindness, goodness, faithfulness, 23 gentleness, and self-control. There is no law against these things!" (NLT)

"But what happens when we live God's way? He brings gifts into our lives, much the same way that fruit appears in an orchard—things like affection for others, exuberance about life, serenity. We develop a willingness to stick with things, a sense of compassion in the heart, and a conviction that a basic holiness permeates things and people. We find ourselves involved in loyal commitments, not needing to force our way in life, able to marshal and direct our energies wisely." (MSG)

Prayer focus for the Day

Dear Lord Jesus Christ live your life through me by the help of the Holy Spirit today in Jesus' name.

20
DEVELOP CONFLICT RESOLUTION STRATEGIES

Conflict is defined as a serious disagreement or argument, typically a protracted one. When a disagreement lingers for too long, it can snowball into a major crisis like bitterness, resentment, outrage and even violence. The word of God is clear on how to deal with it. Ephesians 4:26-27 says, *"And "don't sin by letting anger control you." Don't let the sun go down while you are still angry, for anger gives a foothold to the devil."* (NLT). Anger is one of the emotions given to us by God as humans. It only becomes destructive when it is not well managed. *"Don't let the sun down over your wrath"* is a metaphor to say that you should not have a prolonged anger. Don't give your spouse silent treatment because you are angry. When you do that, you are giving place to the devil in your home. I strongly believe that men as the priests of the house should trust God for grace to initiate reconciliation when the wives are dragging their feet for too long. Don't be like Boaz who was a ruthless business man until he met Ruth.

A woman once gave her husband a silent treatment for a month when the husband excitedly declared in an insensitive sarcasm "...hey, we are getting along pretty well these days." Trust the Spirit of God for humility to initiate the conversation to end the disagreement.

Resolve conflict or disagreement through grace. Pursue your battles wisely. My wife was better than me on this at the beginning of our marriage. I was the bellicose one while she was the peace-loving one. Today we are doing better by God's grace. Peace will always win.

SCRIPTURE OF THE DAY
Hebrews 12:5

"Looking diligently lest any man fail of the grace of God; lest any root of bitterness springing up trouble you, and thereby many be defiled" (KJV)"Look after each other so that none of you fails to receive the grace of God. Watch out that no poisonous root of bitterness grows up to trouble you, corrupting many." (NLT)

"Work at getting along with each other and with God. Otherwise you'll never get so much as a glimpse of God. Make sure no one gets left out of God's generosity. Keep a sharp eye out for weeds of bitter discontent." (MSG)

Prayer focus for the Day

Dear Heavenly Father, I trust you for the abundant supply of grace for today to keep me focused on your love for me and my spouse. No root of bitterness will grow in our family in Jesus' name.

GIVE NO PLACE TO FEAR

Fear is a spirit (Romans 8:15). It destroys, it maims, it should be stopped in its tracks. Fear must never be allowed into your home. It's a spirit that must be attacked when it shows up. You must say NO to fear everywhere. I had a classmate while in high school who was a great striker on my soccer team. His nickname was "NO FEAR." This stuck with him that a lot of people did not know his real name. He was able to intimidate every opposing team in tournaments that he eventually became the highest goal scorer of all time. What I later discovered was that he was not actually the best striker on the school soccer team but the most confident because a man with the name "NO FEAR" must not be seen as a coward.

Do not entertain any fear about your marriage. Do not freak out on any little disappointment. Don't panic. Fear creates crack for the tormentor to come in and oppress you. God's word says fear brings torment (I John 4:10). Fear of separation, divorce, bitterness, death, are all from the devil and they weaken your faith. Fear brings couples into bondage. Say a big NO to fear. Fear allowed is faith contaminated. Fear is destroyed in your home in Jesus' mighty name.

SCRIPTURE OF THE DAY
II Timothy 1:7

"For God hath not given us the spirit of fear; but of power, and of love, and of a sound mind." (KJV)

"For God has not given us a spirit of fear and timidity, but of power, love, and self-discipline." (NLT)

Romans 8:15

"For ye have not received the spirit of bondage again to fear; but ye have received the Spirit of adoption, whereby we cry, Abba, Father." (KJV

"So you have not received a spirit that makes you fearful slaves. Instead, you received God's Spirit when he adopted you as his own children. Now we call him, "Abba, Father."" (NLT)

"This resurrection life you received from God is not a timid, grave-tending life. It's adventurously expectant, greeting God with a childlike "What's next, Papa?" God's Spirit touches our spirits and confirms who we really are." (MSG)

Prayer focus for the Day

Father, in the name of Jesus Christ, we expel every spirit of fear around us. We intentionally walk in our liberty as children of God with sound minds in Jesus' name.

POWER POINT 22

LEARN TO GIVE UP IN ARGUMENTS

LEARN TO GIVE UP IN ARGUMENTS

It is interesting to know the way God measures true spiritual growth. One of them is not in how many arguments we have won with our spouses but how many we have given up for Christ's sake. But when disagreement between you and your spouse is prolonged, it is in your best interest to seek for Godly counsel from trusted people with the following qualities:

They are Jesus Christ focused and they understand God's grace. You don't need legalistic codes at this point.

They are honest and sincerely love you. They don't have to be perfect.

They have been married for a few years ahead of you.

They are sincerely happy in their own marriage.

It could be a great testimony that nobody has ever intervened in your marital challenge before but to die in silence with unresolved crisis just for the sake of bragging right is not wise.

When an argument between you and your spouse is becoming boisterous, give up. The one that gives up is the real winner. Never forget that. It took me a long time to understand this point. Receive grace today in Jesus' name.

SCRIPTURE OF THE DAY

Ephesians 4:26

"Be ye angry, and sin not: let not the sun go down upon your wrath..." (KJV)

"And "don't sin by letting anger control you." Don't let the sun go down while you are still angry..." (NLT)

"Go ahead and be angry. You do well to be angry—but don't use your anger as fuel for revenge. And don't stay angry. Don't go to bed angry. Don't give the Devil that kind of foothold in your life." (Ephesians 4:26-27, MSG)

Prayer focus for the Day

In the name of Jesus Christ, we receive grace and wisdom to resolve every challenge immediately in Jesus' name.

ACCEPT WHO YOU ARE IN CHRIST

Personality type refers to the psychological classifications of different types of individuals. Personality types are sometimes distinguished from personality traits. For example, introverts and extroverts are two fundamentally different categories of people with other categories in between the two. We are all different in the way we are wired or configured.

According to trait theories, introversion and extraversion are part of continuous dimension with many people in the middle. Without going into complex analysis of these temperamental traits, researchers and behavioral scientists have identified four major temperaments credited to a man called Hippocrates, also known as the father of medicine. It is believed that every human being will fall into one or two even three categories of these temperaments. Different recent psychologists and scientists have expanded the study using new terminologies and colors to describe the different classifications of these temperaments. They are as followed depending on your preference for the terms.

1. *Choleric*

    a. STRENGTHS: leadership, confident, ambitious, efficient

    b. WEAKNESSES: demanding, impatient, tense, intolerant

2. *Sanguine*

   a. STRENGTHS: outgoing, optimistic, confident, sociable

   b. WEAKNESSES: selfish, exaggerates, shameless, impulsive, disorganized

3. *Melancholy*

   a. STRENGTHS: considerate, detailed, creative, thoughtful, organized

   b. WEAKNESSES: discontent, pessimist, moody, obsessive

4. *Phlegmatic*

   a. STRENGTHS: calm, diplomatic, rational, reliable, peace-loving

   b. WEAKNESSES: shy, unambitious, apathetic, passive, indecisive

Couples should never have to hide under the guise of temperament as an excuse not to grow. Spirit-controlled temperament is attainable through God's grace. Study Tim Lahaye's <u>Spirit Controlled Temperament.</u> Receive more grace today in Jesus' name.

SCRIPTURE OF THE DAY
Psalm 139:14

"I will praise thee; for I am fearfully and wonderfully made: marvellous are thy works;

and that my soul knoweth right well." (KJV)

"Thank you for making me so wonderfully complex! Your workmanship is marvelous how well I know it." (NLT)

"I thank you, High God—you're breathtaking! Body and soul, I am marvelously made! I worship in adoration—what a creation!" (MSG)

Prayer focus for the Day

Heavenly Father, I receive wisdom to relate and help my spouse's temperament type today in Jesus' mighty name. I also draw strength from the Holy Spirit to deal with my weaknesses as I focus on your love for me in Jesus' name.

MAINTAIN THE SPIRIT OF EXCELLENCE

It is true that beauty is in the eye of the beholder so the saying goes, but it is equally true that ugly things can also be seen by a honest beholder. I personally believe that couples should be very creative about making themselves attractive to each other forever. Excellence is a spirit that couples should walk in all the times in different areas. And that includes cleaning the house, wearing nice clothes, perfumes, deodorants, etc. And you don't have to rob the bank or go bankrupt to do these. You can live excellently within your budgets.

As ministers of the gospel who have been privileged to minister to people across cultures, my wife and I have heard so many things that are responsible for crisis in homes ranging from terrible odors, dirty kitchen, dirty underwear, laziness at cooking, wife watching movies or on social media all day.

Some women also say they can't stand their husband's pot bellies, dirty, hairy armpits, riotous dress sense, mouth odor, etc. The beautiful thing about all these complaints is that none of them is hopeless. The truth is that where Christ is in the center, and people are growing in grace, these challenges can be turned into jokes. For instance, my wife has helped me with my poor eating habit. I gulp food so fast like I am in a war zone because I consider eating a waste of my time. I always want to get back to "meaningful things" (as if food is meaningless). But my wife doesn't think like that. She tried to change me by force at the beginning of our marriage but I rebelled, but when we both started growing in grace we laugh about such things now. I now eat slowly a little bit. Spouses should also believe God for the grace to live with certain non-destructive habits that their partners will not likely change.

For me, my wife may have to live with me eating with a fork on my right hand and knife on the left. That's what is convenient for me. I once told her that I will only change that habit if my life was on the line or a million dollars was on the table as a reward (LOL). Obviously that's not a threat to our marriage. Got the point?

Things that cannot be compromised where excellence is concerned are not limited to smell, the way you talk in public, dress sense, neatness, hygiene, hard work, domestic cleanliness, etc, but the overall excellent spirit in the atmosphere of your home. These simple things have destroyed marriages. Receive wisdom in Jesus Name.

SCRIPTURE OF THE DAY
I Corinthians 14:40

"Let all things be done decently and in order." (KJV)

"But be sure that everything is done properly and in order." (NLT)

"Be courteous and considerate in everything." (MSG)

Prayer focus for the Day

We receive grace to display God's excellent
Spirit in us on a daily basis
in Jesus' mighty name.

MAXIMIZE AND ENJOY THE BEAUTY OF GODLY SEX

Endeavor to build a strong emotional and physical intimacy that leads to sexual fulfillment. It has been said that a good sexual intercourse between a man and a woman binds the soul together. But Godly sex is a union between a male husband and a female wife within a holy matrimony. It involves spirit, soul, and body. It must be mutually enjoyed and held in high honor as a spiritual commitment. Sexual union between a man and a woman in a holy matrimony is a different type of relationship that is different from others. That is why sex with other people or things other than one's spouse of the opposite sex is wrong. It is a sacred union that should be respected. Sex is physical, emotional expression of leaving, cleaving, and becoming one flesh (Genesis 1:27). The sacredness of this act and the spirituality with which it is done is what separates us from animals. God Himself gets satisfied and fulfilled on His throne when it is done the right way because He created it. You should never be ashamed to appear naked before your spouse (Genesis 2:25).

In fact, initiating sex should never be the prerogative of the husbands alone. Wives should never be ashamed to ask for sex from their husbands and vice-versa. You should never deny your spouse or use it as a tool to manipulate each other (I Corinthians 7:5). Apart from the spiritual, emotional and the satisfaction of sexual intimacy, experts are finding out that there are also a lot of medical and psychological benefits. A few of them are listed below.

1. Good, consistent sex boosts the immune system

2. It keeps stress level down

3. It improves women's bladder control

4. It lowers blood pressure

5. Lowers the risk of heart attack

6. Improves libido

7. Lowers the risk of prostate cancer. Research findings published in *American Medical Association Journal* show that men who ejaculate frequently are less likely going to get prostate cancer.

8. It improves sound sleep. After orgasm, the hormone called prolactin is released which enhances sleep.

9. It boosts self-esteem by improving the brain power. It makes analytical thinking more effective.

10. It improves overall physical fitness. It is said that half an hour of sex can burn 144 calories.

11. It enhances your sense of smell which means your nose is healthier.

12. Makes couples look younger. A Scottish study shows that loving, supportive couples who have sexual intercourse three or more times a week appear 10 years younger than their actual ages. This is because

orgasms trigger the release of sex hormone in both men and women which improves the radiance of their skin.

13. It improves tooth health.

14. It lowers risk during pregnancy.

Please note that these are not medical advice from me. These are research opinions. You need to talk to your physician for medical advice.

The point is, sex between a married couple should be enjoyed maximally. People usually ask about the appropriate frequency. I believe it is up to the couple.

There is this funny story that happened in a men's conference. The speaker had just finished explaining the joy that comes with sex and then asked the men how frequently they have intimacy with their wives. Some said "...two or three times a week." Some said "once a week." While the others said "once a month." But one man jumped up with excitement and was screaming "one day in a year, one day in a year, one day in a year." All the men turned around to see this very excited man dancing. "...And why are you so excited and full of life Sir, knowing that you only get to make love to your wife one day in a whole year?" "It is because today is that day." The man responded. The whole room started roaring with laughter. The moral of this story is that sex between a husband and a wife in a Godly marriage is a happy experience. Receive more grace for this in Jesus' name.

SCRIPTURE OF THE DAY
I Corinthians 7:2

"Nevertheless, to avoid fornication, let every man have his own wife, and let every woman have her own husband." (KJV)

"But because there is so much sexual immorality, each man should have his own wife, and each woman should have her own husband." (NLT)

"It's good for a man to have a wife, and for a woman to have a husband. Sexual drives are strong, but marriage is strong enough to contain them and provide for a balanced and fulfilling sexual life in a world of sexual disorder." (MSG)

Song of Solomon 3:4

"It was but a little that I passed from them, but I found him whom my soul loveth: I held him, and would not let him go, until I had brought him into my mother's house, and into the chamber of her that conceived me." (KJV)

"Then scarcely had I left them when I found my love! I caught and held him tightly, then I brought him to my mother's house, into my mother's bed, where I had been conceived." (NLT)

"Restless in bed and sleepless through the night, I longed for my lover. I wanted him desperately. His absence was painful. So I got up, went out and roved the city, hunting through streets and down alleys. I wanted my lover in the worst way! I looked high and low, and didn't find him. And then the night watchmen found me as they patrolled the darkened city. "Have you seen my dear lost love?" I asked. No sooner had I left them than I found him, found my dear lost love. I threw my arms around him and held him tight, wouldn't let him go until I had him home again, safe at home beside the fire." (Song of Solomon 3:1-4, MSG)

Song of Solomon 4:9

"Thou hast ravished my heart, my sister, my spouse; thou hast ravished my heart with one of thine eyes, with one chain of thy neck." (KJV)

"You have captured my heart, my treasure, my bride. You hold it hostage with one glance of your eyes, with a single jewel of your necklace." (NLT)

"Come with me from Lebanon, my bride. Leave Lebanon behind, and come. Leave your high mountain hideaway. Abandon your wilderness seclusion, Where you keep company with lions and panthers guard your

safety. You've captured my heart, dear friend. You looked at me, and I fell in love. One look my way and I was hopelessly in love! How beautiful your love, dear, dear friend—far more pleasing than a fine, rare wine, your fragrance more exotic than select spices.

The kisses of your lips are honey, my love, every syllable you speak a delicacy to savor. Your clothes smell like the wild outdoors, the ozone scent of high mountains. Dear lover and friend, you're a secret garden, a private and pure fountain. Body and soul, you are paradise, a whole orchard of succulent fruits—Ripe apricots and peaches, oranges and pears; Nut trees and cinnamon, and all scented woods; Mint and lavender, and all herbs aromatic; A garden fountain, sparkling and splashing, fed by spring waters from the Lebanon mountains."
(Song of Solomon 4:8-15, MSG)

Prayer focus for the Day

Heavenly Father, my heart is open for the outpouring of your love so I can give from the abundance of your love to my spouse in Jesus' name.

APPRECIATING YOUR EXTENDED FAMILY

One of the major challenges in our world is always the ability to maintain a healthy balance between extremes. It is true that God's word says, *"...a man leaves his father and mother and is joined to his wife, and the two are united into one"* (Matthew 19:5, NLT), but the same Bible also says that God is the creator of the family system. In fact, God is big on genealogy and ancestry.

You both were raised by two different families who invested their lives, time, energy, money and other resources on you. Even though God's word encourages you to leave and cleave for the purpose of becoming one, nowhere in the Bible does God's word say you should outrightly abandon your extended family members. Be kind to each other's family. Give them gifts, visit when you can. Show them respect and love within the boundaries of Scriptures. I know this can be challenging in certain cultures, where extended family members overstep their boundaries by encroaching into your privacy. If this happens, you need to graciously create reasonable boundaries without cutting them off. Jesus wouldn't do that, would He? No. He loves everybody but He did not commit Himself into the hands of no man (John 2: 24-25).

The point is, your extended family members are still part of your social life and you must allow the love of God to flow from you to them without jeopardizing your own immediate family. Receive grace for this healthy balance today in Jesus' mighty name.

SCRIPTURE OF THE DAY
Galatians 6:10

"As we have therefore opportunity, let us do good unto all men, especially unto them who are of the household of faith." (KJV)

"Therefore, whenever we have the opportunity, we should do good to everyone—especially to those in the family of faith." (NLT)

"Right now, therefore, every time we get the chance, let us work for the benefit of all, starting with the people closest to us in the community of faith." (MSG)

Prayer focus for the Day

We are grateful for our parents, brothers, sisters, and other members of our families. We receive wisdom to demonstrate the love of Christ in a way that honors you Lord and protect our marriage in Jesus' name.

UNDERSTANDING THE DIFFERENT FACES OF YOUR SPOUSE

UNDERSTANDING THE DIFFERENT FACES OF YOUR SPOUSE

An average person on earth functions in a complex way that takes a lot of patience and understanding to figure out. I believe God created us that way so that we can keep exploring ourselves in Him in variety of ways. This is not referring to personality disorder which is a mental illness. It is about your different unique sides that are needed for different occasions per time. For example, when a married man is displaying his face of a king which speaks of his God-given authority, his wife must be the queen at this point. There is the face of a lover: the wife must be romantic. There is the face of a friend: the wife must be a friend. And there is the face of a child: the wife must be a mother here. For the woman, she has the face of a queen: the husband must respond like a King. She has the face of a lover: the husband must be romantic at this point. She has the face of a friend: the husband must not be a bully but have fun. And she has the face of a child: the husband must play the role of a father and pamper her at this point.

Crises arise when couples tend to play misfitting roles during these different stages. For example, when your wife puts on her face as a friend and you put on your kingly face, there will be disharmony. Also, when the husband is wearing his kingly hat and the wife is trying to be a lover, there may be a cacophony. It takes a lot of skills, understanding, and discernment through God's grace to be in unity with one's spouse during these different periods. Receive grace today in Jesus' name.

SCRIPTURE OF THE DAY
Psalm 49:20

"Man that is in honour, and understandeth not, is like the beasts that perish." (KJV)

"People who boast of their wealth don't understand; they will die, just like animals." (NLT)

"We aren't immortal. We don't last long. Like our dogs, we age and weaken. And die." (MSG)

Ephesians 5:17

"Wherefore be ye not unwise, but understanding what the will of the Lord is." (KJV)

"Don't act thoughtlessly, but understand what the Lord wants you to do." (NLT)

"Don't live carelessly, unthinkingly. Make sure you understand what the Master wants." (MSG)

Prayer focus for the Day

Dear heavenly Father, I receive fresh grace, wisdom and patience to help navigate through the different unique sides of my spouse in Jesus' name.

28
BE DELIBERATE ABOUT SELF-INVESTMENT

When people hear the word "invest" they quickly assume stock, bonds, real estate, business, etc. While investing in business and enterprise is good for the family, one of the greatest investments of all times is investing in one's self. Some people call it personal development.

If you invest in your career, you will make a profit but if you invest in yourself, you will have a lifetime of fortunes. Investing in your marriage by buying books, resources, and studying them increases your chance of succeeding in an any endeavor including marriage. Buying a book for $25 is not the author's worth, but what has taken him several years and decades to learn. Can you really purchase a 25-year-old marriage experience with twenty-five dollars? Don't you think that is actually a massive discount? I bet you do. Unfortunately, today, we have a generation of whiners who would rather be on social media all day and just walk past the resources table at conferences. And we wonder why an average marriage collapses within 2 years. That will not be your experience in Jesus' name.

SCRIPTURE OF THE DAY
II Timothy 2:15

"Study to shew thyself approved unto God, a workman that needeth not to be ashamed,

rightly dividing the word of truth." (KJV)

"Work hard so you can present yourself to God and receive his approval. Be a good worker, one who does not need to be ashamed and who correctly explains the word of truth." (NLT)

"Concentrate on doing your best for God, work you won't be ashamed of, laying out the truth plain and simple." (MSG)

II Timothy 4:13

"The cloke that I left at Troas with Carpus, when thou comest, bring with thee, and the books, but especially the parchments." (KJV)

"When you come, be sure to bring the coat I left with Carpus at Troas. Also bring my books, and especially my papers." (NLT)

"Bring the winter coat I left in Troas with Carpus; also the books and parchment notebooks." (MSG)

Prayer focus for the Day

Heavenly Father, open my eyes of understanding as we behold Jesus Christ in all of the resources available to us so we can apply the knowledge gained from them as a family in Jesus' name.

UNDERSTANDING THE STATE OF ABSORPTION

God is the ultimate, best matchmaker. He not only knows our past, but our present and future. When couples don't quit too soon because of a few challenges, their past and present challenges, personal idiosyncrasies and habits (good or bad) can actually be merged with that of their partners to form a strong coalition. It has been discovered that couples who hang on in their marriage after a while start absorbing their partners' values, characters, and even personality traits. They start laughing alike, and behaving alike not because they are trying to imitate each other but because they are simply obeying a basic rule of human psychology and neuro chemistry which says we are exceptionally good imitators.

The longer couples stay together, the deeper the *emotional contagion*. This is a term in psychology which describes a process by which many of us grow to feel the same emotions as those around us, particularly our spouses and friends. This empirical study is so practical that I see it in my relationship with my wife and our friends. Debby and I now think alike on major issues, laugh alike, and even speak alike on certain occasions. This is called language style matching (I Corinthians 1:10). Psychologists are simply using cozy words *(emotional contagion)* to describe Amos 3:3 which states, **"Can two walk together, unless they are agreed?"** (NKJV).

In fact, after a few years in marriage, couples begin to notice an exchange of personality traits. The one that is an extrovert becomes more reserved and the introvert begins to speak out more. It is a healthy situation because it means covenant is practically becoming a reality. In ancient cultures, strengths and weaknesses were exchanged when covenants were cut. When you notice these changes, you should not be alarmed, let them flow as long as those exchanges are positive and are bringing more life and vitality into your marriage. I believe God allows this to happen to avoid boredom. It is part of growth and transformation from glory to glory. Receive more grace to enjoy your new self in Jesus' mighty name.

SCRIPTURE OF THE DAY

Corinthians 3:18

"But we all, with open face beholding as in a glass the glory of the Lord, are changed into the same image from glory to glory, even as by the Spirit of the Lord." (KJV)

"So all of us who have had that veil removed can see and reflect the glory of the Lord. And the Lord—who is the Spirit—makes us more and more like him as we are changed into his glorious image." (NLT)

"And so we are transfigured much like the Messiah, our lives gradually becoming brighter and more beautiful as God enters our lives and we become like him." (MSG)

Prayer focus for the Day

Dear heavenly Father, I trust you with my life as I behold the face of Jesus Christ for my transformation from glory to glory through the help of the Holy Spirit in Jesus' mighty name.

GO AFTER GODLY MENTORS AND ACCOUNTABILITY PARTNERS

GO AFTER GODLY MENTORS AND ACCOUNTABILITY PARTNERS

The importance of mentors and accountability partners cannot be overemphasized. Your progress in life is as good as the people you surround yourself with. Surround yourself with people who are going in the same direction as you maritally: It is a known truth and a fact that your associations and friendships can to a large extent determine where you are headed in life. Interestingly, our heavenly Father will not leave us without a witness. If you are humble enough, you will identify people who are more experienced in what you are trying to accomplish. Especially those who are truly following Christ. Connect with them and listen to them. I Corinthians 11:1 says, *"And you should imitate me, just as I imitate Christ."* (NLT). Also Titus 2:3 talks about the importance of Godly mentoring from older women, *"Similarly, teach the older women to live in a way that honors God. They must not slander others or be heavy drinkers. Instead, they should teach others what is good."* (NLT). Unfortunately, most couples hang out with sycophants who will tell them what they want to hear. It is very imperative that you are in the circle of those who honor the sanctity of marriage and they are living it out. A research was carried out recently which says if a friend divorces, the odds of getting a divorce by the friends of the divorcee increase by 33%. Which means divorce can be contagious. The research shows a clear effect of divorce. It falls under the category of *"social contagion."* When couples pursue divorce, others in their social circle tend to perceive it as an indirect permission to do the same. Therefore, surround yourself with people who are ready and willing to help you "fight" for your marriage with prayers, Godly counsels, community support systems, etc.

Sometimes, life challenges and situations may tend to make us think that we are alone in our struggles. The moment we get into this mindset, our circumstances are exaggerated beyond measure and the desire to pursue a solution is shut down. But when we humbly submit to Godly counsel from experienced mentors, we stand a better chance to navigate through the learning curve gracefully.

Usually, many of the things that cause crisis in marriages are the very things that God wants us to help each other resolve through His grace. Matured, Godly mentors have a way of showing people that their spouses are not enemies, but allies that have been sent to help in the battles of life. May your steps be ordered to identify Godly spiritual authority today in Jesus' name.

SCRIPTURE OF THE DAY
Philippians 4:9

"Those things, which ye have both learned, and received, and heard, and seen in me, do: and the God of peace shall be with you." (KJV)

"Keep putting into practice all you learned and received from me—everything you heard from

me and saw me doing. Then the God of peace will be with you." (NLT)

"Summing it all up, friends, I'd say you'll do best by filling your minds and meditating on things true, noble, reputable, authentic, compelling, gracious—the best, not the worst; the beautiful, not the ugly; things to praise, not things to curse. Put into practice what you learned from me, what you heard and saw and realized. Do that, and God, who makes everything work together, will work you into his most excellent harmonies." (Philippians 4: 8-9, MSG)

Prayer focus for the Day

Heavenly Father, I receive grace to attract Godly mentors into my life who will help me in my relationship with my spouse in Jesus' mighty name.

CONSIDER INTELLIGENT SEPARATION WHEN YOUR LIFE IS IN DANGER

There is no doubt that the marriage institution is under a vicious attack and people get hurt daily. Spousal physical, and emotional abuses and violence are real issues happening every day to real people. Where this happens regularly, seek help before your spouse kills you. It takes people who are alive to be married. We have heard stories of couples killing themselves. I counsel married couples who are consistently violent to consider intelligent separation after which they prayerfully seek Godly counsels to see if they are both willing to make the marriage work through God's grace. Outright divorce should be the last option. I strongly believe that there should never be a divorce until all the options have been exhausted including counseling sections for a long period of time (different sessions). The word of God says *"...no longer will violence be heard in your land..."* (Isaiah 60:18).

Unfortunately, a lot of couples are not willing to go through counseling. Refusing to submit for counseling is especially common for men. The reason for this could be traditions, cultures, shame, ego, or outright arrogance. In any case, there is nothing inherently wrong with counseling especially from matured, experienced, Godly couples. Receive wisdom today in Jesus' mighty name.

SCRIPTURE OF THE DAY
Proverbs 3:29

"Devise not evil against thy neighbour, seeing he dwelleth securely by thee." (KJV)

"Don't plot harm against your neighbor, for those who live nearby trust you." (NLT)

"Don't figure ways of taking advantage of your neighbor when he's sitting there trusting and unsuspecting." (MSG)

Prayer focus for the Day

We resist every temptation to talk violence, act violently, or get involved in any disrespectful manners towards each other. We declare peace on our home in Jesus' name.

LEARN TO CREATE SPACE FOR YOUR SPOUSE

Unity in marriage is a legitimate experience that every honest couple desires. While it is attainable, but you must understand that unity can also be a paradox. This is because God wants the couple to explore life together without destroying their uniqueness and personal interests. The whole idea that the only life's purpose of a woman is to support her husband's vision is not only childish but a convoluted opinion of an oppressive system which is a product of lack of understanding of God's heart for creating man. When the Triune God said *"...Let us create man in our image..."* that included the female gender. When you study it in context, Man here refers to the 8 billion people on earth today, members of the human race. Pay attention to these words *"let them have dominion over the fish..."* Genesis 1:27. God created man (humanity) male and female. Verse 28 says *"And God blessed them."* The point here is: both the man and the woman have equal right where the relationship with God and dominion is concerned. Therefore, there are times when the couple may need some personal time to enjoy their individuality. Marriage should never destroy that *me alone moment.* It took me a while to understand this marriage-saving principle. Occasionally, I take our children out for hours, maybe to restaurants or movie theaters just so that my wife can be alone and have her own alone time. She humorously told me one time that she enjoys her "peace and space" when I travel for speaking engagements. The truth is that I enjoy being alone in moments like that also. It helps me to focus. The beautiful thing is that we still communicate regularly during these periods. When I am in my writing zone, I ask for my wife's understanding because I know I would withdraw into my space.

Essentially, creating space for your spouse so that he or she can focus on God's purpose is not a bad idea. In fact, it creates more joy and a sense of "I have missed you bonding." Life can be boring when it is monotonous and predictable. Again, when the focus is on Christ, you will find out that no human being completes you better than Jesus Christ. May the Lord give you understanding in Jesus' name

SCRIPTURE OF THE DAY
I Corinthians 7:5

"Defraud ye not one the other, except it be with consent for a time, that ye may give yourselves to fasting and prayer; and come together again, that Satan tempt you not for your incontinency." (KJV)

"Do not deprive each other of sexual relations, unless you both agree to refrain from sexual intimacy for a limited time so you can give yourselves more completely to prayer. Afterward, you should come together again so that Satan won't be able to tempt you because of your lack of self-control." (NLT)

"Abstaining from sex is permissible for a period of time if you both agree to it, and if it's for the purposes of prayer and fasting—but only for such times. Then come back together again." (MSG)

Prayer focus for the Day

Dear heavenly Father, I receive your miraculous wisdom and grace to allow my spouse to fulfill Your purpose for his/her life in Jesus' mighty name.

POWER POINT 33

BE SECURED IN GOD'S LOVE AND REST IN HIS GRACE

BE SECURED IN GOD'S LOVE AND REST IN HIS GRACE

Inadequate self-image and insecurity can be dangerous if left unchecked. It can lead to destructive obsession, anger, jealousy, and other negative emotions in the realm of the soul. There is this story of a man who went shopping in a big store with his insecure, jealous wife. After one hour of shopping, he couldn't locate his wife at this huge store. Then he remembered his old trick, the man approached a very beautiful woman and appealed to her to engage him in discussion for a few minutes. "Why" the woman asked. "Because every time I talk to other beautiful women, my wife suddenly appears out of nowhere."

Insecurity can also be worse for men who are not growing in God's grace. It's not just about women. A very elderly couple was having an elaborate dinner to celebrate their 75th wedding anniversary. The old man whispers softly to his wife "sweetie, our sixth child doesn't really look like the rest of the children. I promise that nothing will ruin this celebration if your answer is what I'm thinking about. Did he have a different father?" The wife dropped her head and paused for a few seconds unable to look at her husband. "Yes" she says. With tears in the eyes of this terrified old man, he asks "who? who was he? Who was his father?" Again, the woman drops her head for a few seconds as she tries to muscle the courage to say something soberly "You honey." The old man felt bad and embarrassed. Isn't it amazing that some men still cannot trust their wives even after 75 years of marriage. (LOL).

The morale of these two stories are:

Rest in God's grace and entrust your spouse into the hands of God in prayer. Husband and wife must be able to have open communication on issues with a view to helping each other. God's grace is sufficient for you today in Jesus' name.

SCRIPTURE OF THE DAY
Hebrews 4:16

> "Let us therefore come boldly unto the throne of grace, that we may obtain mercy, and find grace to help in time of need." (KJV)

> "So let us come boldly to the throne of our gracious God. There we will receive His mercy, and we will find grace to help us when we ne it most." (NLT)

> "So let's walk right up to him and get what he is so ready to give. Take the mercy, accept the help." (MSG)

Prayer focus for the Day

We receive a fresh revelation of your love.
We bask in the glory of your grace that is
capable of destroying every insecurity
in Jesus' name.

34
BE ALERT IN THE SPIRIT

Marriage is doing life with your spouse. Therefore, exploring life in the Spirit is a lifetime journey that makes you see things beyond the natural. And this includes marriage.

While I am not recommending that you go spooky and phony in an attempt to be spiritual, it is also important to be spiritually sensitive. God may want to show you a deeper thing beyond the ordinary that can help you in your relationship that experts may not be able to understand. Sometimes, your heavenly Father may just inspire you to do ordinary things in an extraordinary way using a divine approach. For instance, God said to me one day while working late in my office, "Call your wife now and tell her how much you love her." I had said that a thousand times before but because it was a divine instruction, I obeyed God and something broke loose in the realm of the Spirit that space will not allow me to talk about.

A word came one day to a lady in our church. She had unknowingly offended her husband and this had made the husband shut down emotionally. She believed that the word was for her and she went home to ask her husband for forgiveness after which the man wept like a baby. That was the beginning of a new honeymoon to this day.

Operating at the supernatural frequency of the Holy Spirit

cannot be overemphasized. Marriage is a faith journey. It is a great and a glorious risk as long as you embark on the adventure in the spirit of grace. Don't despise supernatural intervention.

SCRIPTURE OF THE DAY
Galatians 5:16

"This I say then, Walk in the Spirit, and ye shall not fulfil the lust of the flesh." (KJV)

"So I say, let the Holy Spirit guide your lives. Then you won't be doing what your sinful nature craves." (NLT)

"My counsel is this: Live freely, animated and motivated by God's Spirit. Then you won't feed the compulsions of selfishness. (MSG)

Prayer focus for the Day

We receive grace to consistently walk in the Spirit in Jesus' mighty name.

EPILOGUE:
A WORD FOR THE SINGLES, WIDOWS, WIDOWERS AND SINGLE PARENTS.

It has been an amazing journey on MARRIAGE MAKEOVER. That you made it to this point is an indication that you are committed to your spouse and the marriage institution. Thanks a lot.

However, while researching and writing this book, I thought about the different categories of people who may be thinking if this book is really for them. They are the divorcees, the single parents, the widows and widowers, the celibates, and those who are not interested in marriage.

Well, the brutal truth is that not everyone will marry in this world. May be because they are not interested or may be because they can't just seem to find the right person on time and now they are old and are no longer interested. If you are in this category, don't feel bad. Nothing is wrong with you and you should never allow the definition of success according to your culture to hurt you. More on this in my next book for the singles.

For the widows, widowers, divorcees, single parents out there who will like to marry again, do not let any man made doctrine of fear hold you bound. Nobody died for you on the cross except Jesus Christ. I find it absurd that God will still throw somebody to hell fire to roast for all eternity because the sin of divorce is so great that the blood of Jesus cannot cover that one. But a man and his wife may patch things in their troubled marriage of hell on earth and occasionally have side chicks. The same doctrine that demonizes divorcees believes that adultery can be forgiven but divorced people who remarry cannot move close to the gates of heaven. This is ludicrous

If you think I am supporting divorce, you may need to read this book over and over again from the beginning. I am actually tenaciously anti-divorce. And I will remain so till I see Jesus by God's grace. My wife and I, with our ministry leadership, have sat down with distressed couples for countless hours sometimes 8 to 10 hours at a sitting. So I know the potential horrors of divorce but to banish and stigmatize divorcees is not only tragic, it is almost blasphemous. It's like saying Jesus Christ did not do a good job. My dear brothers and sisters who are separated or divorced, Debby and I are standing with you in prayers for healing and restoration. Our miracle working God can bring you and your ex together, if they are still available, but if you decide to move on with another God-fearing person, you will not go to hell because of that. Just focus on Christ and His finished work of grace this time around and fulfill your purpose which is the primary reason for marriage in the first place.

Be on the lookout for my book on how to attract the right person. It's a book for the singles, single parents, widows, and widowers. The Bible is clear on these subjects. Receive the peace of God that passes all understanding through our Lord Jesus Christ. Love you.

REFERENCES

1. America Medical Association Journal
2. Akinmola, Bankole: Understanding God's purpose for your marriage
3. Dollar, Creflo: The Successful Marriage
4. Evans, Jimmy: Marriage on The Rock
5. Chapman, Gray: The 4 Season of Marriage
6. Munroe, Myles: Understanding Love
7. Okonkwo, Kingsley: A-Z of Marriage
8. Ore, Sam: Towards A Purposeful Marriage
9. Wikipedia

Contact Information

SAM ORE

Kingdom Ambassadors Christian Center

Email: Pastor@KACConline.org

Website: www.samoreministries.org, kacconline.org

Please include your testimonies or help received from reading this book. You prayer requests are also welcomed. You can order additional copies of this book or any other by the author at

www.amazon.com

www.samoreministies.com

or simply send an email to pastor@kacconline.org with your request.

www.ingramcontent.com/pod-product-compliance
Lightning Source LLC
Chambersburg PA
CBHW070912160426
43193CB00011B/1439